# Swimming Home

Susan Hand Shetterly

Illustrations by Rebekah Raye

In celebration of all the people in coastal towns who are working to bring back their fish runs.

TILBURY HOUSE PUBLISHERS · THOMASTON, MAINE

**Pesca** raced through the ocean with the other alewives in her school as winter winds whipped the water into steep waves and sleet fell. They were hunting tiny animals that drifted in clusters, sometimes near the surface of the water and sometimes deeper where the light was dim.

The alewives swam fast and close together. Often they looked like one big fish flashing silvery scales, but they were many fish with gray-green backs, silver bellies, and sharp tails. Behind the curve of their gill covers, on each side, they were marked with a small, dark spot.

When spring came and the full moon shone down, shadows of birds moved across it. The birds were flying north.

Pesca and her school felt something pulling them. It was Lily Lake, where they had hatched from eggs in water that was not salty like this ocean water, but sweet and muddy.

The year before, in a springtime much like this one, Pesca, the oldest and biggest alewife, had led her school back to Lily Lake to spawn, their eggs drifting down to the bottom.

Now she would do it again.

Slowly they turned and headed north with the birds, as alewives before them had done for thousands of years. They joined other schools of alewives, making one enormous, glittering school.

Ahead of them, going the same way, raced a pod of porpoises. A humpback whale rose out of the water and splashed down as they hurried beneath its huge shadow. But soon Pesca and her school left the other alewives and swam on their own toward a cove where the familiar smell of Lily Lake wound through the water like a wide ribbon.

A boy, out with his father in a rowboat, leaned over the side and noticed sudden bright, bold flashes of silver—first one, then another—and then the dark backs.

"Dad!" he said. "The alewives are here!"

They watched a harbor seal chase the fish. Pesca and her school dashed from the seal and flashed past the rowboat, tracking that ribbon of lake water to the mouth of Lily Stream.

To reach Lily Lake, the alewives would have to fight their way up the stream, flooded with snowmelt and spring rain, but they weren't quite ready to enter it yet. When they came to it, they circled back into the cove.

"Years ago, when your grandfather was a boy," the boy's father said as he rowed,
"he'd come to Lily Stream in May with a dip net and fish for alewives with his dad.
They'd salt them and put them into a smokehouse they built on the bank right over
there. They used woodchips to make the smoke. Your grandfather said nothing
tasted as good as a freshly salted and smoked alewife."

"Why don't we do that?" the boy asked.

"There aren't enough left anymore. Now every fish that returns needs a chance
to spawn."

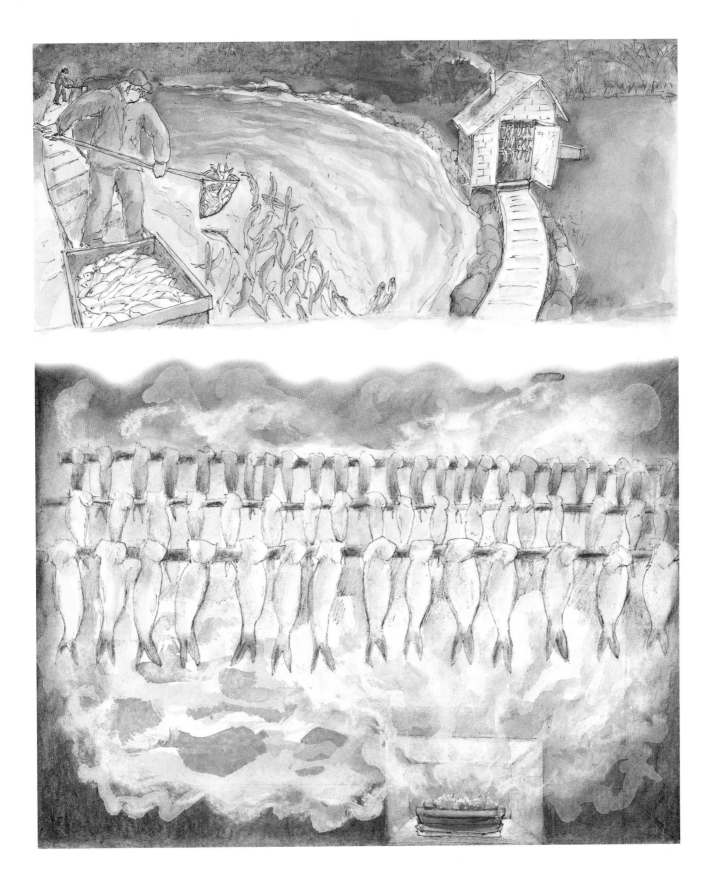

The next day, when the tide was high and the salt water in the cove rose against the water of the stream, the alewives were ready.

Pesca plunged in, ducking between two giant rocks. She shimmied one way. She shimmied another. The other alewives followed beside her. Up they went, darting past rocks and sunken logs.

When one of them spotted a bald eagle flying overhead, he swerved behind a log, and all the other alewives scattered and hid.

The bird dropped from the sky. It splashed into the stream and rose again, its talons empty. It shook itself and flew away, and the alewives continued their journey.

Once Pesca hung in a slow eddy between two sticks. But they were not sticks. They were the long, thin legs of a great blue heron.

When the bird saw Pesca, it stabbed its beak into the water. Just before it grabbed her, she shot upstream again.

The alewives arrived at a deep pool. They would not eat while they made their way to Lily Lake, but here they rested, fanning their tails back and forth in the quiet water.

Then they began again, and didn't stop until they reached a beaver dam that stretched from bank to bank before them.

Over the top of the dam skimmed a sheet of water, and water poured through gaps where branches and stones and mud had come loose.

One by one, thrashing their tails, the alewives turned sideways and skimmed over the top, or they wriggled through the open spaces in the dam.

They swam slowly in the beaver pond beside the round dome of the lodge. Two beavers sat on the lodge gnawing the bark of green saplings and watching the fish as rain began to fall. Raindrops puckered the surface of the water.

Night fell. The rain slowed, then stopped.

A barred owl called Who-WHO-who-who-aaah.

When the sun rose, the alewives started upstream again. Ahead of them, they heard a clattering noise that shook the banks. As they got closer, the sound grew louder.

A brand-new road ran across Lily Stream. Over it, cars sped. Under the road a pipe lay on a pile of stones. The lovely water of Lily Lake poured through it and splashed down into the stream. The people who had set the pipe under the road had forgotten about the alewives.

The fish shimmied and jumped.

They slid and skidded.

They somersaulted and back-flipped.

But they couldn't reach the pipe.

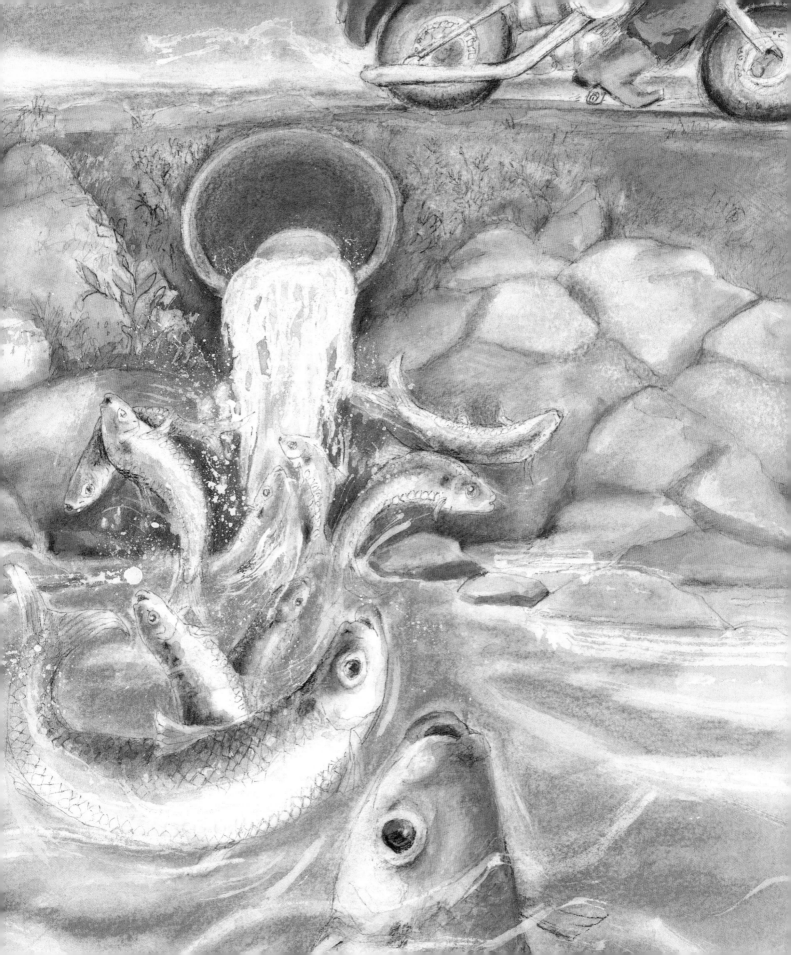

Pesca and her school had come a long way. They had escaped the seal and the bald eagle and the great blue heron. But if they couldn't swim through that pipe, they couldn't get to Lily Lake, though it was just on the other side of the road.

Pesca rushed again at the falling water. It tossed her back.

She tried again.

This time the water flipped her sideways into a puddle on the bank. Another alewife fell next to her. They twisted and flapped, but they were stuck.

That was when the boy and his father who had seen the alewives in the cove came walking along the streambank looking for the fish.

"There they are!" said the boy. "But the pipe's too high for them."

"Let's help. These two first," said his father. "Get your hands wet so you don't hurt their skin. And be careful—people don't call them sawbellies for nothing! The scales on their bellies are sharp."

The boy dipped his hands into the stream. Gently, he lifted Pesca and carried her across the road. He held her in the water of the lake.

Pesca moved a little. She took a breath. Then another. She fanned her tail back and forth. She felt a surge of life, twisted out of the boy's hands, and darted away as the alewife who had fallen beside her swam from the father's hands.

Together the two alewives circled back as the boy's father ran to get buckets.

He and his son began to scoop up other fish, carrying them across the road and pouring them into the lake. Back and forth they went, scooping and pouring, as more and more alewives gathered next to Pesca. Soon every fish in the school was safe in Lily Lake.

When they finished, the boy and his dad sat by the shore. They looked out over the water. They couldn't see the alewives, but they knew the fish were there.

"The trouble is, more will be coming," the father said, putting his arm around his son's shoulders. "I'm not sure what we'll do about them."

"Neighbors will help us," the boy said. "We can all bring buckets to carry the alewives across the road."

"That's a good idea. You know, we saved some special fish today, and I bet right now they're celebrating."

The boy laughed. "Dad, do fish really celebrate?"

Just then Pesca broke the water's surface in a flash of the most beautiful silver. She flipped her tail high like the wave of a hand and disappeared with all the other alewives deep into Lily Lake.

## AUTHOR'S NOTE

Pesca and her alewives will stay to spawn in

the lake. Then, once more, they will

find the stream. They will float through

the pipe to the stream below, over or

through the beaver dam, into the cove,

and out into the ocean.

Next year, when the fish return, the boy and

his father and their neighbors may have

built a fish ladder and set it into the pipe

for the alewives to rise, step by step,

through the water coming down.

Alewives are members of the herring family. They live in the western North Atlantic Ocean. People are not sure how these fish got their name. The best guess is that they somehow reminded European settlers on this coast of the wives of tavern keepers back in Britain. They are also called "river herring" because they swim up rivers and streams to their home ponds and lakes to spawn.

When they swim from salt to fresh water or from fresh to salt, their bodies have to adjust. In salt water, they drink constantly and absorb water through their skin and gut while expelling salt from special filaments on the undersides of their gills. In fresh water, instead of drinking, they get rid of as much water as they can through their kidneys.

Fish that move from salt water into fresh water to spawn are called "anadromous." The word comes from Greek and means "running upward." A possible advantage for alewives of spawning in freshwater ponds and lakes is that there may be fewer predators there than in the ocean. But this migration may also be the result of changes in the land and water brought on by the last Ice Age, which forced fish from fresh water into brackish and then salt water. Those that survived this change may have established a pattern of returning to their original habitat for reproduction.

Mature alewives are about 11 inches long and weigh about 9 ounces. Females carry up to 100,000 eggs. When the fish reach their spawning grounds, the males and females gather close together, thrashing in the water and releasing the eggs and the clouds of milt that fertilize them.

After spawning, the adult fish drift back to the bays and feed ravenously, then return to the open ocean. An individual fish may make the spring run three or more times beginning in its third or fourth year. Some returning alewives swimming upriver in the spring may be eight years old or older, but most of the fish are four years old, and making the run for the first time.

In Maine the beautiful fish begin to enter their home rivers in May. As the season warms and water temperatures rise, the older, returning fish arrive first, followed by those that are migrating upstream for the first time tracking the scent trails of the fish ahead of them.

Young fish hatch from the eggs left behind and spend their first summer feeding on freshwater zooplankton, growing to five inches long. When they begin to move downstream to the saltwater bays, people call them flippers, because this is the only stage in an alewife's life when it jumps.

Adult alewives are deep from back to belly but thin from side to side. They swim with sudden bursts of speed. Because of their slimness, they can easily swim upstream through water coming down.

In Maine, alewives were once harvested in spring in every town that had a fish run. They were used for food—as salted and smoked fish—and as bait to be stuffed into mesh bags that were then set into lobster traps. A town would license one of its citizens to take a certain number of fish, and the town kept a share of the money that was made when the fish were sold.

Traditionally, widows of the town were presented with two free bushels of alewives every year.

Today only a few towns have alewife runs plentiful enough to harvest.

Alewives once occurred in huge numbers along our East Coast. There are stories of them schooling so thickly in the bays that it looked as if a person could walk from shore to shore across their backs. But over time the numbers of fish dropped and the much-celebrated runs died away. Culverts built under roadways stopped the fish. So did dams. So did pollution. All sorts of impediments put into rivers and streams were often good for people but bad for the fish. And alewives were overharvested for years.

Recently, scientists have discovered that one reason for the plunging numbers of cod, pollock, haddock, bluefish, and other species of finfish along this coast may be the decline of the alewife runs. Now people are studying the relationship between these fish and the once-plentiful alewives.

Recent restoration of fish passage in Maine has allowed more than two million alewives to swim up the Sebasticook River. The famous Damariscotta River run provides a weir and pool system for about 900,000 fish. Here in my hometown of Surry, we are working to restore the alewife run in Patten Stream, a small, swift stream out of lower Patten Pond. We are hoping for a run of 250,000 fish a year when the work is done.

TILBURY HOUSE, PUBLISHERS
12 Starr Street, Thomaston, Maine 04861
800-582-1899 · www.tilburyhouse.com

First hardcover edition: September 2014 · 10 9 8 7 6 5 4 3 2 1

ISBN 978-0-88448-354-0

Visit the
Tilbury Learning Center
for more!

I dedicate this book to the members of the Surry Alewife Committee; and to Nate Gray, Theo Willis, Ted Ames, and Claire Enterline for their scientific help; to my son, Aran, for his essential and thoughtful edit; and to the memory of Melissa Laser, gifted biologist. —SHS

For my favorite swimmer and so-talented sister, Patricia A. Bradley. A special thank you to my mother Frankie E. Bradley and my friends Daryl DeJoy and David Wilkins, who work tirelessly to protect all creatures and their environments. And a big thank you to my husband, Ken Woisard, whose patience, love, and sharing fuels the place I need to be when I work and play. —RR

Library of Congress Cataloging-in-Publication Data

Shetterly, Susan Hand, author.
Swimming home / Susan Hand Shetterly ; illustrations by Rebekah Raye. —First hardcover edition.
     pages cm
Audience: K to grade 3.
ISBN 978-0-88448-354-0 (hardcover : alk. paper)
1. Alewife—Behavior—Juvenile literature. 2. Animal migration—Juvenile literature.  I. Raye, Rebekah, illustrator. II. Title.
QL638.C64S54 2013
597.45—dc23                          2013038248

Book design by Geraldine Millham, Westport, MA; cover design by Kathy Squires, Newburyport, MA.
Printed by Pacom Korea, Inc., Kyunggi-do, Korea; 2014.